Threatened Species

Written by Steve Parker
Illustrated by David Marshall

© 1993 Henderson Publishing Limited

THREATENED SPECIES

A great sadness of our age is that around the world, so many wonderful animals and plants are in danger of disappearing for ever. They are beautiful, fascinating, awe-inspiring, useful, even dangerous. Like us, they have a right to live their lives, and share the world.

How to help
It's an enormous tragedy. For some, it is too late. But all is not lost. The more we discover and learn, then the more we will know what to do, and how to help. That's the reason for writing this book. The animals can't tell you, so we will. You can find ways to help at the back of the book.

Threats galore
Many threats face animals and plants.

1. **Hunting** Great whales were driven to the edge of extinction for their meat and oil. Will they recover?
2. **Poaching** Gorillas, our close cousins, strong and intelligent, are killed for their hands, feet, teeth and skulls. Rhinos are poached just for their horns.

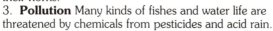

3. **Pollution** Many kinds of fishes and water life are threatened by chemicals from pesticides and acid rain.
4. **Habitat destruction** This is the biggest single danger. Giant pandas just about hang on as their patches of Chinese cloud forests get smaller, taken for farmland and villages.
5. **Even tourism**! Monk seals and turtles, the last of their kind, may lose out on the Mediterranean beaches.

WHAT'S A SPECIES?

Before finding out about threatened species, we should ask — what is a species?

It's a group of animals that can breed together, with each other, but which cannot breed with any other kind. A species is the basic unit or group in nature. Lions, tigers, cheetahs and leopards are all separate species.

Once the last members of a species are lost from the world, that species can never come back.

How many species?
There are probably more than 10 million species in the world. Less than two million have been fully identified and described by scientists.

Yet thousands, perhaps millions, are in danger of disappearing for ever. A small book like this can only list a few hundred.

Even familiar animals that we see in zoos and parks are becoming rare in their natural homes.

What does "endangered" mean?

Scientists use several terms to describe the level of threat to an animal or plant species. These terms are found in the official lists and books of species under threat.

Rare Early warning! The species is not endangered — yet. But there aren't many of them.

Vulnerable Later warning! The species looks as if it will become endangered, unless it gets help.

Endangered Latest warning! The species is so rare that it will become extinct if nothing is done to save it.

Extinct Too late. If a plant or animal hasn't been seen for 50 years, it is said to be extinct. That's it. Gone for ever.

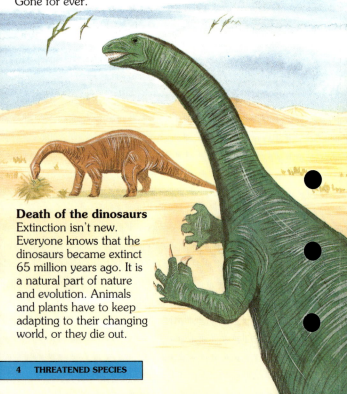

Death of the dinosaurs
Extinction isn't new. Everyone knows that the dinosaurs became extinct 65 million years ago. It is a natural part of nature and evolution. Animals and plants have to keep adapting to their changing world, or they die out.

Keeping up

For thousands of years, people have used plants and animals and their bits for food, clothing, building materials, tools and decorations.

A long time ago, there were not so many people. They used animals and plants slowly. Most of the animals and plants grew again. They were 'sustainable resources'.

Today it is different. Some plants and animals are being used faster than they can replace themselves.

Losing out

In the past, extinctions were few. New species had time to evolve, to take the place of the lost ones.

Today, we are killing off animal and plant species at a mind boggling rate. Evolution cannot keep up.

Between 1800 and 1850, about 10 bird and mammal species became extinct. More than 150 have already gone this century.

How many in danger?

No one really knows how many species are under threat today. But the estimate is pretty gloomy. It could be one species every day, probably more.

By the year 2000, our world may have lost 50,000 kinds of plants and animals.

MAMMALS IN PERIL

Many animals have been killed because of fear. People thought wolves, bears and tigers would eat them, their children and their farm animals. Snakes and spiders would, it was thought, poison them as they slept.

In fact, most hunting animals, left alone in their natural homes, leave people well alone.

Shoot out
The grey or timber wolf lived with the great herds of American bison, eating old and sick animals. But when the settlers killed the bison, the wolves had nothing to eat but the settlers' cattle. So the settlers declared war on the wolves.

Now wolves are very rare across large areas of North America.

Red peril
The American red wolves did even worse. People killed them until they were almost extinct. Then they realised what was happening. The few surviving red wolves were rescued, to breed in captivity. They have now been released into suitable wild places.

THREATENED SPECIES

Adaptable bear

- Spectacled bears of South America eat almost anything edible and live almost anywhere. A recipe for success, would you think?

- No. People have killed most of these magnificent creatures. The bears will not breed in captivity. So the only way to save them will be by legal protection.

Wanted, dead or ... dead?

In the days of the Wild West, the cougar or mountain lion had a price on its head. People were frightened of it.

- These beautiful animals were shot on sight, and the US government paid a reward or bounty. The last bounty was handed over in 1890. But the hunters missed a few animals. Luckily. Today there is a healthy population.

Tigers at risk

For the old-time big game hunters, the tiger was the greatest 'prize'. People paid huge sums to go on a tiger hunt and kill one of these magnificent beasts, the biggest of the big cats.

But in 1970, worried people counted only 5,000 tigers left in the forests of Asia. One of the world's most famous animals was facing extinction. Hunting was banned and tiger reserves were set up.

Too successful

Project Tiger was generally successful. Today, there are more tigers than the reserves can hold.

But over-crowded tigers are very dangerous. They prey on farm animals and threaten local people. More reserves are needed, or tigers will again be killed.

THREATENED SPECIES 7

Dog days are numbered

The African hunting dog may not be everybody's favourite animal. It is killed by farmers protecting their livestock. It is also affected by diseases such as canine distemper, anthrax and rabies.

It's a dog's life, and these fascinating pack-hunters are under threat.

No bats in the belfry

Many people are frightened of bats, simply because we don't understand their mysterious ways and night-time swoopings. But bats are one of the main groups of animals in deadly danger. There are 950 species around the world, but there could soon be fewer. Why?

Too tidy

Modern tidiness is partly to blame. People chop down old trees and knock down old buildings, which are the roosting sites that bats used for years. Church belfries are covered by nets. Caves become tourist attractions. Modern buildings have no entry holes to their lofts.

Pesticide chemicals kill the bats' insect food, and poison the bats themselves.

Trying to help

In Indiana, USA, almost half a million bats used to hibernate in some special caves. But 60,000 of them died when tourists came to look at one of the caves, and woke the bats from their sleep. Next, well-meaning people blocked the entrance to a second cave, to keep the tourists out. The blockage also kept out fresh air. Another 80,000 bats perished.

Batty British bats

European horseshoe bats feed on insects, often swooping down and picking them off the ground. They roost in trees and buildings by day, and hibernate in caves in the winter.

All European horseshoe bats are endangered. In Britain, more than nine-tenths of the lesser horseshoe bats have disappeared in the last 100 years.

One thing leads to another

Egyptian fruit bats had a great time when people started growing fields of fruit. But the fun was short-lived. The bats soon became pests. They were trapped, shot and poisoned. However, the efforts to get rid of the fruit bats had other effects. They led to the virtual extinction of eight smaller species of insect-eating bats.

Slow to recover
Pig-like tapirs are very tasty meat, so they have been hunted almost to extinction. Their Malayan forest homes are disappearing, too. These shy, nocturnal animals are struggling to survive.

Catch me a colobus
Many species of colobus monkeys live in African forests. Local people call any animals that they can eat 'bush-meat'. Colobus are good bush-meat. These lively monkeys are now endangered.

Disappearing grace
For thousands of years, great herds of antelopes on the dry lands of northern Africa have provided people with meat and skins. But now, domestic cattle get the meagre grazing. Among the endangered species are the scimitar-horned oryx, addax, Dama gazelle and slender-horned gazelle.

Working through history
Asian elephants have worked for people for 5,000 years. There are now very few truly wild elephants left. The forests where they live are shrinking. They have nowhere to hide from the poachers who kill them for their ivory tusks.

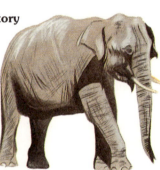

One hump or two
Even the familiar camels are in trouble. There are no wild dromedary (one-humped) camels left in the world. And there are only a few hundred wild bactrian (two-humped) camels in central Asia. All the other camels are domestic (tame) ones, or their descendants.

FUR AND FASHION

- People have always used animal skins to keep warm. But then they invented 'fashion'. They wanted to look as good as the most beautiful animals. Then some animals, especially the elegantly spotted small cats, got rarer and rarer. There was an outcry. Surely no one really needed to hunt and kill these wonderful creatures, just for the sake of their own vanity?

- **Protected at last**
  Today, the trade in many animal furs is illegal. The legal trade in furs is also much smaller. Many creatures, such as mink, are specially bred on farms to give up their coats.

- **Fur farming**
  Chinchillas have long, soft, silver fur. It keeps them warm in the high Andes mountains. For centuries, people killed them for this beautiful fur.

Luckily, these cute animals live happily in captivity. They are now bred on farms. So the few remaining wild chinchillas should be safe. (If it wasn't for the poachers.)

- **Two fatal features**
  Giant otters from South America are playful, curious animals with luxurious furry coats. They also have no fear of humans — which makes them very easy to catch. The fur and fearlessness are two fatal features. These animals, two metres long, are hunted mercilessly. They now survive only in tiny, undisturbed patches of Amazonian forest.

Double trouble

The beautiful snow leopard was hunted for its skin. Now the wild mountain sheep, its main food, are disappearing because of the spread of farm animals. So the snow leopard is fast disappearing, too.

Stripy problem

How can the great herds of zebra wandering across our televisions be endangered? The most elegant species, Grevy's zebra, has been ruthlessly hunted for its skin. These animals also have to compete with domestic cattle for grazing and water.

The other panda

Lesser or red pandas, from the Himalayan region, are not close relations of their giant black-and-white namesake. But they are almost as threatened. Shy and nocturnal, they are hunted for their soft fur, and also caught to sell as pets.

Eager beavers

During the 1700s and 1800s, beavers were hunted almost to extinction for their fur, by the trappers in Canadian forests.

Nature experts then realised that not just the beavers were missing. Without their tree-felling and dam-building, many wetland plants had gone. So, for several reasons, the beavers are back!

Cotton-tops

Not only fashion and the pet trade threaten animals. Thousands of cottontop tamarins were taken from their Central American forest homes. Many died on the journeys. Some became pets. Others were used for medical research.

Scaly medicine

The scales of the strange pangolin are made of pressed-tight hair, like the horn of a rhino. These scales are used in recipes for some Oriental medicines. Pangolins are also easy to catch. And their meat is tasty. Needless to say, there are now few left.

Horns for handles

A single rhino horn is worth as much as £50,000. The horns are ground into powder for traditional medicines, or carved to make dagger handles for kings and princes. So poachers kill rhinos, take their horns, and leave the bodies to rot.

African rhinos

Twenty years ago, there were nearly 30,000 black rhinos roaming across southern Africa. Now there are only about 3,000, restricted to a few game reserves.

Southeast Asian rhinos

The Sumatran rhino, the smallest of the five rhino species, does not live in protected areas. It is in critical danger. There are only two small groups of the once-common Javan rhino. They are unlikely to survive.

Indian rhinoceros

In India, rhinos have been well protected in parks and reserves. Now there are too many! It is hoped that they can be re-introduced to areas where they once lived.

Elephant problem

Poachers kill African elephants at the rate of about 70,000 each year. All they want is the ivory tusks. The rest of the carcass rots. At this rate, all African elephants will be dead by the year 2000. It is difficult to protect these huge beasts. They have gigantic appetites and need vast areas to live in, which are difficult for the anti-poaching guards to patrol.

THE DEATH THREATS

- Any type of human activity that harms a natural place is a threat to endangered species. We don't have to hunt the animal directly. Cutting down the woodland where it lives is just as bad. How would you like to come home and find your house and street flattened into a car park?

- ### Man the hunter
  People began to hunt very early in our history. They learned to use weapons, and became so good that they started to cause extinctions. The woolly mammoths of the Ice Ages may have been some of the first to go at the hand of Man. Today their cousins the elephants are under similar threat.

- ### Habitat destruction
  This threat is the BIGGIE. The modern world is changing much faster than ever before. People are turning wild, natural lands into fields for crops, pasture for farm animals, roads and motorways, quarries and factories, offices, houses and shops, leisure centres ... the list is almost endless. As the natural places are destroyed, so are the plants and animals that live there.

- ### Wood you credit it?
  Woodland is a valuable resource. Timber is needed for building houses and bridges, making furniture, and as firewood for heating and cooking. Millions of people around the world burn wood every day. They must get it from somewhere. The problem is that woodlands, especially in the tropics, are very rich in animal and plant life.

Pollution

Poisonous chemicals used in agriculture and industry get into the waterways, and harm the plants and animals.

Toxic chemicals buried in land dumps seep into the soil and poison plants and creatures. Or the chemicals drift into the air and make acid rain. Or they destroy ozone and cause the Earth to heat up, and expose living things to dangerous radiation.

There is hope

Slowly, people are realising that we must protect our planet. Governments are making laws to stop factories releasing poisonous chemicals, to stop trade in endangered animals and plants, and to protect them in national parks. People are buying things made by recycling, and in ways that are sustainable. You reading this book shows that you care!

Competition

Otters and seals were hunted because they ate the fish that people wanted to angle for, or eat themselves. There are many cases of competition between wild animals and us.

RIVERS AND SEAS

- Rivers and lakes are under threat because of acid rain. Pesticides and other chemicals seep from fields into them, and poison the wildlife. Fertilisers do the same, and upset the balance of nature. Even the sea, once so wide and clean, has become a global dustbin for raw sewage, rubbish and toxic chemicals.

- **Seal story**
  Seals are great swimmers, but they cannot run very fast. So they are easy to catch on land. Hundreds of thousands have been killed for their fur, and because they eat the fish we want to catch. Many seal species are in danger of becoming extinct.

A dying habit
There were once three species of monk seals. Fishermen thought the seals damaged their fishing nets and are 'their' fish, and so ignored campaigns to save them.

- The Caribbean monk seal is already extinct. Nine-tenths of the Hawaiian and Mediterranean monk seals have died.

  Seal of success
- In 1892, there were only about 100 northern elephant seals. They became a protected species. Today there are
- 65,000 of these huge, noisy beasts. They are an exciting tourist attraction.

THREATENED SPECIES

Dugongs and manatees
These huge, gentle sea mammals eat underwater plants in rivers and along the sea shore. If they are not killed for meat, oil and skins, they are in further danger from fishing nets, water pollution, and the whizzing propellers of power boats. The whole of Florida is now a manatee refuge.

The right one
The right whale swims slowly at the surface, and it does not sink when it dies. Ideal for whaling! So it was considered the 'right' whale to hunt, and that's how it got the name. Along with the blue whale, bowhead and humpback, it is endangered. There are only a few thousand left.

Saving the whales
Whales were killed for their meat and oil until they reached the edge of extinction. Now there is an international ban on whaling.

Recent discovery
The smallest and most endangered 'small whale' is the Gulf of California porpoise, or vaquita. It was only discovered in 1958. Now it gets trapped in fishing nets and, being an air-breathing mammal, it drowns.

DISAPPEARING HOMES

The giant panda of China is perhaps the most famous endangered species. It eats only bamboo. But its bamboo forest homes are being cleared for farms, villages and firewood. Many scientists and the Chinese government are trying to save the giant panda.

Love corridors
In the hilly forests, panda sanctuaries are joined by wooded 'corridors' of lowland, so that the pandas can visit each other to mate.

London Zoo is one of the zoos around the world that is trying to get pandas to breed.

Poor old man
The orangutan is the second largest of the great apes, and extremely endangered. Its name means 'old man of the forest'. But the forests in question, in Borneo and South-East Asia, are disappearing fast.

Gruesome trade

Gorillas are gentle, social animals from rainforests in West and Central Africa. Yet their forest homes are disappearing. Horribly, poachers kill them to cut off their hands and feet, to sell as 'souvenirs'.

There are still several thousand of the lowland gorilla species. But there may only be about 300 mountain gorillas left.

Indri lemurs are almost extinct. They survive partly because local people think they are the ghosts of their ancestors, and so do not harm them.

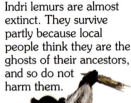

Grubby fingers

One of the strangest creatures of Madagascar is the shy, nocturnal, lemur-like aye-aye. Scientists thought that it was extinct. Luckily it was only hiding. The aye-aye eat grubs that it pokes from under tree bark with its super-long middle fingers. However, trees are being cut down, and the aye-aye is in peril.

Ghostly survivors

When European people first discovered Madagascar, there were over 40 species of monkey-like lemurs. Today there are only about 20 species, and most of these are endangered.

Too close to Rio
Tiny monkeys called lion tamarins live in dense vines in Brazilian rainforests. There are only a few hundred left and they live dangerously close to the rapidly expanding city of Rio de Janeiro.

Spiny anteater
Echidnas are unusual mammals because they lay eggs. They don't like to live near people, because they get hunted for meat. Even in Australia, there are not many places left for them to hide.

The numbat is back
Many of Australia's unusual mammals live nowhere else in the world. Since Europeans arrived, at least 18 species have disappeared. The hairy-nosed wombat, the bridled nail-tail wallaby and the greater stick-nest rat are almost extinct.

Monkeys going bananas
Squirrel monkeys live in the Central American forests. Their trees are being felled to make way for fields of rice, sugar cane and banana trees. The monkeys now live in a reserve in Costa Rica.

The numbat is a ray of hope. It has been protected and re-introduced into places where it once lived.

THREATENED SPECIES 21

BIRDS ON THE BRINK

Birds are killed for meat, eggs, feathers — and fun. Every year thousands of bird species migrate in huge flocks. In some places the flocks pass through 'bottlenecks', such as the Straits of Gibraltar, or a valley between high mountains. Human hunters lie in wait and blast them out of the sky.

In the Mediterranean area alone, 10 million people kill 1,000 million birds every year, for 'sport'.

Cranes of the plains
In 1941, only 15 whooping cranes flew past hunters waiting for them, as they migrated across North America's Great Plains to Texas. Numbers are slowly rising after a desperate campaign to stop the crane killing.

Can't win
Despite EC protection, the peat-bogs of northern Britain are being turned into bags of potting compost and sold in garden centres. The rare Greenland white-fronted geese can no longer use these traditional places for spending the winter. So they take refuge on neighbouring farmland. The farmers shoot them.

22 THREATENED SPECIES

Gull eats gull

Audouin's gull is one of the world's rarest gulls. The Mediterranean islands where it breeds are nature reserves. The problem is herring gulls, those well-known and numerous pests. They eat all the natural food and also Audouin eggs.

Like the glaucus macaw, the little Spix blue macaw is probably extinct in the wild. There are 20 captive birds, but they don't realise the problem, and they refuse to breed.

'Who's an endangered boy, then?'

Millions of parrots have been taken from the rainforests, especially in South America, and put into cages as pets.

There are only a few thousand hyacinth macaws left in the wild, and 60 indigo macaws.

Humming to extinction

Each species of tiny, buzzing hummingbird is designed to drink nectar from one type of flower. The birds carry pollen to fertilise the flowers. So as the forests and flowers are cleared, the hummingbirds are homeless.

THREATENED SPECIES

Keep looking

The fabulous harpy is the world's largest eagle, with a body a metre long and a wingspan of more than two metres. It swoops on monkeys, opossums and other prey.

This great bird lives between Mexico and Argentina — but only where the rainforest is completely undisturbed. As you might guess, it is very rare.

Dedicated dad

The male cassowary sits on his eggs for as long as 48 days without moving, to hatch them. Yet there are very few wild cassowaries left in Australia. Hunting, forest destruction, disease and road accidents have killed them.

Disappearing compost heaps

The mallee-fowl is another attentive bird father, carefully adjusting the temperature of the eggs in their compost-heap incubator. The Australian mallee, or scrubby land, is being turned to farmland and the mallee-fowl have nowhere else to go.

THREATENED SPECIES

No state bird

The Californian condor is the bird symbol of the USA's California state. When people came to the mountains to look for gold, they hunted the animals that the condors normally fed on. More recently, condors have died after feeding on poisoned carcasses.

Californian condors became extinct in the wild when the last few sick birds were captured, as an attempt to save them. In the early 1990s, the total population was in the 30s.

Ex-kiwis

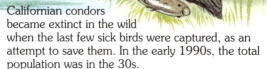

The kiwi may soon be the ex-national bird of New Zealand. These famous flightless birds are suffering from habitat loss. All three species are threatened.

Selfish holidaymakers

From 1900, you could no longer shoot the North American piping plover. But the birds lay their well-camouflaged eggs on pebbly beaches — where people take their holidays!

By 1987, there were less than 500 pairs of these birds. Now, the beaches are closed during the plover's breeding season. Yet people protest against the closed beaches. They want their holidays!

Peregrine peril

DDT is a chemical that farmers used to spray on their crops, to kill insect pests. Mice and voles ate the crops and took in the DDT. Peregrine falcons ate the mice and voles, and did the same. The DDT makes birds' eggshells very thin, and the chicks died. The peregrine falcon became extinct in the USA, before DDT was finally banned.

Stolen eggs

Great Indian bustards are magnificent birds. Standing over a metre tall, they weigh 14 kilograms. The thorn scrub where they nest is being turned into farmland. When they do find a place to nest, someone steals their eggs for collections.

Don't shoot

Probably just 2,000 pairs of black vultures are left in the world. Many of them live on a huge area of land in Spain. The landowner has stopped the Spanish airforce from making a shooting range there, to protect the birds.

Feather fashion

In the last century, short-tailed albatrosses were very popular — as feathers on ladies' hats! By 1953, there were only 10 pairs of these wonderful wanderers left. Fortunately fashions changed and the birds survived, just!

REPTILES, AMPHIBIANS & FISH

Turtles, crocodiles and similar creatures have been around since before the dinosaurs. But the days are numbered for many of them. People can do in less than a century, what nature could not do in 200 million years — drive them to extinction.

Walking meat store
Galapagos giant tortoises were used by old-time sailors as living fresh-meat stores. Many kinds are in great danger.

Turtle tale
Six of the seven species of sea turtles are in trouble. They are hunted for meat, leather and oil. They drown in fishing nets, and they choke on plastic rubbish and tar, which they mistake for food.

Hatchling mistake
The beaches where the sea turtles lay their eggs are being taken over by holidaymakers. And turtle eggs are dug up and eaten as a delicacy — by lizards and foxes, as well as people. Any baby turtles that hatch head for the bright lights of the roads and discos, instead of to the sea.

Confrontation

30 years ago, 3,750 loggerhead turtle nests were found on one Israeli coast. In 1991, there were two! Local people would rather have the holidaymakers and their money, rather than protect the turtles. Can we blame them? If your livelihood was in danger, what would you choose? Job or turtle?

Turtle soldiers

In Mexico, the beach nesting sites of sea turtles have an armed guard, to stop people killing the turtles for meat and taking their eggs.

Living fossils

Tuatara lizards live on New Zealand islands. They have survived since the days of the dinosaurs. But only just. Now they dwell on a few island sanctuaries where there are no cats, dogs and rats — yet.

Most dangerous croc

Estuarine or saltwater crocodiles spend most of their time in coastal waters, around the Indian and west Pacific Oceans. They have been virtually exterminated for their skin, and because they are so big and dangerous. Now the killing and skin trade is strictly controlled.

From handbags to pets
American alligators were almost wiped out because people made handbags and shoes from their skins. In the 1960s, laws protected them. They have recovered, almost too well. They eat the occasional family dog, and escaped alligator pets have become a problem in some city sewers.

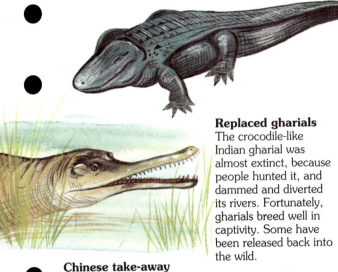

Replaced gharials
The crocodile-like Indian gharial was almost extinct, because people hunted it, and dammed and diverted its rivers. Fortunately, gharials breed well in captivity. Some have been released back into the wild.

Chinese take-away
High in the Chinese mountains lives the world's largest newt, the Asian giant salamander, nearly two metres long. Unluckily, it is a great Chinese delicacy, and it is becoming rarer.

Olm home

The olm is a strange salamander found only in a few European caves. It is blind and colourless and never grows out of its 'tadpole' stage. Water pollution and changes in river systems are its big threats.

Three-pond frog

The Cape Platanna frog is now found in only three ponds, in the Cape of Good Hope nature reserve of South Africa. The waterways where it used to thrive have been drained, filled in or polluted.

Biggest newt

In Britain, the great crested newt is the biggest newt, at 16 centimetres long. It is very rare and protected. People guard the few ponds where it lives.

Peter Pan pet

The strange axolotl is a salamander that never grows up. It always seems to look like a tadpole. It is often kept as a pet, but its native home is Lake Xochimilco in Mexico. The wild axolotl is not coping well with introduced predatory fish and pollution.

Jaws in danger
The star of the big screen, the great white shark, is an endangered animal. Shark-fishermen have hooked, harpooned and shot it almost out of existence.

Fenced fish
There only 125 Devil's hole pupfish left, in a pool in Ash Meadows, Las Vegas. The pool is surrounded by a high fence with a locked gate. Other pupfish pools have been drained or polluted.

Dammed catfish
The giant catfish can grow to three metres long and 300 kilograms in weight. But such huge specimens are rarely found today. These fish are caught for food, and their migration routes along Chinese rivers are blocked by dams.

Dynamite dinner
In the Amazonian rivers live the huge arapaima fish. People catch them by dynamiting the water, because they are so good to eat. These giants get rarer every year.

THREATENED SPECIES

CREEPY-CRAWLIES

Insects are the most successful animal group on earth. They have been around for hundreds of millions of years, and there are more of them than any other kind of animal.

Scientists already know more than one million species of insects. Almost every day, they discover new species in places like the rainforests. Also every day, great areas of rainforest are destroyed. Thousands of insects and other species probably become extinct, before they were even discovered!

Butterfly giant
The largest butterfly in the world is the rare Queen Alexander's birdwing. Although it is protected by international law, the small area of Papua New Guinea forest where it lives, is not.

Butterfly collectors
Like bird eggs, butterflies are collected by unthinking people. The rarer they are, the more valuable they become. Even though butterfly farms can supply most needs, illegal dealers still catch wild butterflies.

Not just the rainforests
Even in Britain, there are plenty of endangered insects and other animals. The large tortoiseshell and heath fritillary butterflies, and the fiery clearwing and transparent burnet moths, are among them. Nearly a quarter of British dragonfly species, such as the Norfolk hawker and the dainty damselfly, are in danger of disappearing.

Beetle parents
Giant carrion beetles used to live across the USA. They are very good parents, carefully tending and buzzing at their young, as these develop in a rotting animal carcass. Now the giant carrion beetles survive only on Rhode Island.

Taking the medicine
Before modern drugs, doctors used the medicinal leech to suck blood from sick people. So many leeches were used, that today they are rarely found in ponds and rivers.

Robbed of robbers

Robber crabs live among the coconut palms of Pacific islands. They are the largest land animals without a backbone, with legs a metre across. They are rare because island people eat them, use them for fishing bait, and sell their dried bodies to tourists.

Spider pets

Many people keep red-kneed tarantulas as pets. Back home in Mexico, no one knows how many are left.

Last stronghold

Britain's largest spider is the great raft spider. It lives only in a damp fen in Norfolk. Its water is being pumped away to irrigate fields and supply houses and factories. The spider's raft may soon be marooned for ever.

Damaged reefs

Giant clams, the largest shellfish in the world, live on coral reefs in the Pacific Ocean. Like the coral around them, they are taken as tourist trophies or damaged by sight-seeing skin-divers.

PLANTS IN DANGER

Our world has more than 300,000 species of plants. One in ten is threatened by the activities of people. Most of these plants have not been studied by scientists. We may never know if they could produce valuable foods, drugs, oil or other useful substances.

Wonderful forests
Tropical rainforests contain more plants and animals than anywhere else on Earth. They are being cut down for wood and to make way for agriculture. An area the size of 70 football pitches disappears every minute.

Treasures sold off
Orchids and bromeliads (air-plants) are taken from Amazon forests, for sale as houseplants. Trees like mahogany are felled for timber. But most of the forests are cleared for banana and oil-palm plantations, and for cattle who become hamburgers.

Aging instruments

The Chilean false larch grows in Chilean rainforests. Its wood is used for musical instruments, among other things. These trees could be harvested and replanted — except that they take 500 years to grow!

It's a puzzle

The familiar monkey puzzle tree also grows in the Chilean Andes rainforest. Forest clearance threatens them. So do people who carve them into trinkets for tourists.

World's worst stink

The famous Rafflesia plant is a parasite. It sucks sap from vine roots. It has the largest flower in the world, and the stinkiest! It smells of rotting flesh, to attract flies that pollinate it. Yet the vines on which it grows are disappearing, and collectors dig up this world's biggest flower.

In double trouble

Have you ever seen a double coconut? Probably not, because the trees that produce them are very rare. They grow mainly in the Seychelles, even though their coconuts — which are their giant seeds — have been washed up on shores all over the world.

Sweet harmony

Hawaiian honeycreeper birds have beaks specially shaped to sip nectar from certain types of hibiscus flower. As they feed, the birds carry pollen from flower to flower, to fertilise its seeds. Birds and flowers depend on each other. Both are becoming rare.

PLANTS WE NEED

About half of our modern medicines came originally from plants. So did many everyday items such as ropes and cloths. Not to mention highly nutritious foods, packed with vitamins and minerals. How many helpful plants are becoming extinct around the world, year by year?

Too rare to test
The Madagascan periwinkle plant contains over 50 chemicals which may be useful as medicines. It has close relatives that may be even more useful. But there are not enough plants left to test.

Bark medicine
The African cherry is a relative of the cherry tree. A chemical in its bark helps to cure disease. But the tree's survival is threatened, because so much bark is exported to Europe.

Gardener's favourite
European ladies-slipper orchids are so beautiful that people want them growing in their gardens. So they dug them from the wild and took them home. Now these pretty plants grow wild mainly in parts of the Alps.

Too poor for music
The African blackwood is one of the best woods for making clarinets. But any wood is firewood for the poor people of Africa. The only trees that remain are too small and stunted for musical instruments.

Insects for lunch
Pitcher plants live in swamps where the soil is poor. They trap insects in their 'pitchers', for extra nourishment. People like to watch these fascinating plants catch and digest their victims. So pitcher plants are collected, and now hard to find in the wild.

Record breakers

The giant redwoods or sequoias of California, USA, are the largest living things on earth. The forests where they grow were made into national parks, to protect them.

Cactus-rustlers

Anyone who has grown cactuses for a hobby, knows how fussy they are. In Texas, cattle-rustlers have become cactus-rustlers. Species like the Nellie Cory cactus and the saguaro cactus are very rare in some areas.

Popular plant
The African violet is loved by pot-plant enthusiasts and grown in many colours. Yet it is just about extinct in its native home, because of collecting and habitat destruction.

Old roots, new route
Only two patches of the pretty yellow-robin's cinquefoil were left in North America, after the settlers had cleared the forests. One was right in the middle of the Appalachian Trail. So the ancient path was re-routed to stop tourists trampling the tiny plants.

Temple treasure
The gingko tree is a 'living fossil'. Its remains have been found in rocks over 250 million years old. It was saved from extinction because it was treasured in Japanese and Chinese temple gardens.

Scrap the dam
The furbish lousewort stopped a dam being built. Scientists thought that this tiny plant was extinct. Then someone found a patch, growing just where a large dam was to be built, in North America. The dam plan was scrapped.

SAD TALES & SUCCESS STORIES

Extinction is final. There is no going back. However, more and more people are caring about endangered animals and plants. Many scientists, conservationists, politicians and world leaders are trying to turn the tide.

Gone for ever
Steller's sea cows were discovered in 1741 by sailors hungry for fresh meat. By 1800 these huge, gentle marine mammals were gone.

Huge flocks of passenger pigeons darkened the skies of the American Midwest. Millions were shot for food. The last one, Martha, died in Cincinnati Zoo in 1914.

The Irish elk disappeared at the hands of hunters, 600 years ago. This magnificent animal had antlers over three metres across.

- The thylacine or Tasmanian wolf was the marsupial version of the wolf. There has been no trace of this creature in its native Tasmania since the 1950s.

- The quagga looked like a zebra at the front and a donkey at the back. It lived in herds in southern Africa. The last one died in Amsterdam Zoo in 1874.

- And of course, the dodo. This large flightless bird was a relative of our pigeons. It lived on islands in the Indian Ocean such as Mauritius. By the early 1700s, it was gone — truly as 'dead as a dodo'.

Back from the brink

European settlers in North America massacred the bison. Only 800 animals survived in Yellowstone National Park. Now there are 30,000, living in parks and reserves.

The Euro-bison or wisent roamed northern Europe in huge herds. But hunters shot every one — apart from those in zoos. They have been carefully bred and released into the Polish forests of Bialowieza.

The Arabian oryx seemed almost extinct several years ago. A few were captured and bred. They were released and now live happily in Oman.

The pretty Pere David's deer is a popular animal in parks and zoos. It became extinct in the wild of northern China, its natural home. However, there were enough captive animals to re-establish a healthy wild herd.

In the 1970s, there were only five black robins left in New Zealand. The Wildlife Service stepped in and now there are more than a hundred birds.

Vicunas, which are South American hump-less camels, were killed for their soft wool and meat. By 1965, only a few thousand remained. Now protected, their numbers have recovered to nearly 100,000 animals.

THREATENED SPECIES 45

WHO CARES?

Several organisations try to protect endangered animals and plants. Everyone can help by supporting and joining them.

Ways to save wildlife
Create more protected sites, wildlife havens, nature reserves, national parks, game parks and similar areas.

Enforce the laws that stop people building, farming, mining and damaging these places.

End the unfairness of famine around the world. Then people will not have to chop down trees, gather rare plants and hunt rare animals, just to survive.

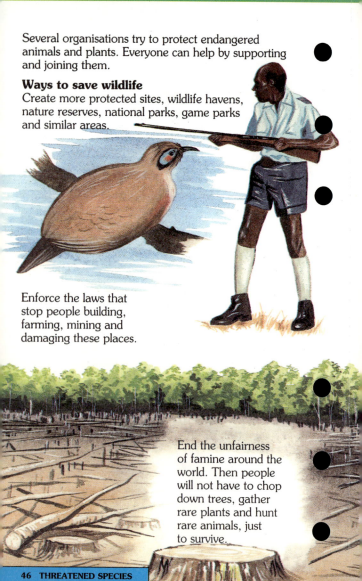

THREATENED SPECIES

Work against pollution and chemicals that spoil the countryside.

Stop the trade in collecting, and in endangered species and their parts — from the rhino's horn and the big cat's coat, to the corals and shells that people buy as souvenirs.

Buy things that are recycled, that are environment-friendly, that come from sustainable resources, and that are generally 'green'.

Spread the message by starting at home. Join a wildlife group. Do projects. Send letters. Start clubs. Get recycling.

THREATENED SPECIES 47

USEFUL NAMES

IUCN
The International Union for Conservation of Nature and Natural Resources is a worldwide organisation that promotes and encourages the protection and sustainable use of living things. It publishes the official Red Lists and Red Data Books of threatened species.

CITES
The Convention on International Trade in Endangered Species is pa treaty that has been signed by the leaders of over 90 countries. It stops wild animals and plants, and their skins, teeth, seeds and other parts, from being sold and traded.

WWF
The World Wide Fund for Nature works to save endangered species and natural wild places.

FOE
Friends of the Earth campaigns and lobbies governments and institutions, to protect the environment.

Greenpeace
An action group that tries to prevent the destruction of wildlife, particularly marine animals.

Lynx
This organisation persuades people to stop buying or trading furs.

Watch
A group especially for young people, part of Britain's Royal Society for Nature Conservation. It aims to educate, and to protect the countryside and its wildlife.